A POSTCARD BOOK™

RUNNING PRESS ♦ PHILADELPHIA, PENNSYLVANIA

Postcard Book is a trademark of Running Press Book Publishers.

Canadian representatives: General Publishing Co., Ltd., 30 Lesmill Road, Don Mills, Ontario M3B 2T6. International representatives: Worldwide Media Services, Inc., 115 East Twenty-third Street, New York, New York 10010.

9   8   7   6   5   4   3
The digit on the right indicates the number of this printing.

ISBN 0–89471–806–1
Cover design by Toby Schmidt
Interior design by E. Michael Epps
Cover illustration: *At the Circus,* 1976, by Marc Chagall. The Estate of Chagall, St. Paul de Vence (Scala/Art Resource, New York). Back cover illustration: *Madonna of the Village,* 1938–42, by Marc Chagall. Thyssen-Bornemisza Collection, Lugano (Scala/Art Resource, New York). Title page illustration: Self Portrait 1959–68, by Marc Chagall (Russian, 1887–1985). Uffizi Gallery, Florence. (Scala/Art Resource, New York).

Typography by Commcor Communications Corporation, Philadelphia, Pennsylvania.
Printed and bound in the United States of America.
This book may be ordered by mail from the publisher. Please add $2.50 for postage and handling for each copy. *But try your bookstore first!* Running Press Book Publishers, 125 South Twenty-second Street, Philadelphia, Pennsylvania 19103.

In the 97 years of his prolific lifetime, Marc Chagall witnessed the tumult of a century: an earthshaking revolution, two world wars, and the birth of the nuclear age. Yet Chagall—as observer, participant, and artist—chose not to make his an art of cataclysm. His luminous paintings and stained glass images glow with brilliant colors; his angels and acrobats leap with exuberance, grace, and balance; even his images of the atrocities of war are counterbalanced by symbols of hope.

At the center of Chagall's art is his belief in the unity of the human experience—that the culture of the past is linked with the present and that the diverse traditions of the world's many cultures can find common ground. The role of the artist is to help viewers recognize symbols and beliefs shared by others around the world.

Born in 1887 in the provincial Russian town of Vitebsk, Chagall received a good part of his early training in St. Petersburg. He soon realized that he should continue his studies in Paris, the center of artistic innovation. In France, Chagall began to view his native land anew:

> In Russia my pictures were without light. Everything in Russia is dark, brown, gray. Arriving in France, I was struck by the iridescence of color, the play of lights, and I found what I had been blindly seeking, the refinement of paint and of wanton color.

Chagall returned to Russia during the turbulent years of war and revolution between 1914 and 1922, and served for a time as Commissar of Art in Vitebsk, among other assignments. But he was drawn back to France, where he once again immersed himself in the "freedom-light" of Paris.

In Paris, Chagall juxtaposed familiar symbols and images with "alogical" settings. His intention was to integrate. In his paintings, he brought together fiddlers, lovers, animals, and peasants remembered from his native Vitebsk; fables from the biblical past, played out in the landscape of the present; and Russian Orthodox icons, which he used as a framework to depict themes of everyday Jewish life in a peasant village. In this way, his lovers take flight over a starry nightscape, a white heifer plays a golden violin as a Jew sits in prayer, and Christ's crucifixion is set against the violent backdrop of a pogrom.

Through these images, Chagall urged his viewers to look beyond the separate components of his work to see an integrated whole. If we do, we can begin to see the richness of distinct traditions as well as a universal reality.

The Green Mare

1911, by Marc Chagall (Russian, 1887–1985). Tate
Gallery, London. (Tate/Art Resource, New York).
Copyright 1990 ARS N.Y./ADAGP

The Cattle Dealer

1912, by Marc Chagall (Russian, 1887–1985).
Kunstmuseum, Basle. (Scala/Art Resource, New York).
Copyright 1990 ARS N.Y./ADAGP

The Poet Reclining

1915, by Marc Chagall (Russian, 1887–1985). Tate
Gallery, London. (Tate/Art Resource, New York).
Copyright 1990 ARS N.Y./ADAGP

Double Portrait with Wine Glass

1917, by Marc Chagall (Russian, 1887–1985). Musée
National d'Art Moderne, Paris. (Scala/Art Resource,
New York). Copyright 1990 ARS N.Y./ADAGP

Peasant Life

1925, by Marc Chagall (Russian, 1887–1985). Albright-
Knox Art Gallery, Buffalo, New York. Room of
Contemporary Art Fund, 1941. Copyright 1990 ARS
N.Y./ADAGP

The Rooster

1929, by Marc Chagall (Russian, 1887–1985). Thyssen-Bornemisza Collection, Lugano. (Scala/Art Resource, New York). Copyright 1990 ARS N.Y./ADAGP

Dream of a Summer's Night

1939, by Marc Chagall (Russian, 1887–1985). Musée de Peinture et de Sculpture, Grenoble. (Scala/Art Resource, New York). Copyright 1990 ARS N.Y./ADAGP

Bouquet with Flying Lovers

1934–47, by Marc Chagall (Russian, 1887–1985). Tate
Gallery, London. (Tate/Art Resource, New York).
Copyright 1990 ARS N.Y./ADAGP

Madonna of the Village

1938–42, by Marc Chagall (Russian, 1887–1985).
Thyssen-Bornemisza Collection, Lugano. (Scala/Art
Resource, New York). Copyright 1990 ARS N.Y./ADAGP

The Juggler

1943, by Marc Chagall (Russian, 1887–1985). Private
collection, New York. (Giraudon/Art Resource, New
York). Copyright 1990 ARS N.Y./ADAGP

War

c. 1943, by Marc Chagall (Russian, 1887–1985). Musée
National D'Art Moderne, Paris. (Scala/Art Resource,
New York). Copyright 1990 ARS N.Y./ADAGP

Lovers and Daisies

1949–50, by Marc Chagall (Russian, 1887–1985).
Private collection. (Art Resource, New York). Copyright
1990 ARS N.Y./ADAGP

Bird and Flowers

1952–56, by Marc Chagall (Russian, 1887–1985).
Private collection. (Bridgeman/Art Resource, New York).
Copyright 1990 ARS N.Y./ADAGP

Moses Before the Burning Bush

1958–60, by Marc Chagall (Russian, 1887–1985). Musée
National Message Biblique Marc Chagall, Nice. (Art
Resource, New York). Copyright 1990 ARS N.Y./ADAGP

The Bride and Groom

by Marc Chagall (Russian, 1887–1985). Private
collection. (Bridgeman/Art Resource, New York).
Copyright 1990 ARS N.Y./ADAGP

The Song of Songs IV

1958, by Marc Chagall (Russian, 1887–1985). Musée
National Message Biblique Marc Chagall, Nice. (The
Granger Collection, New York). Copyright 1990 ARS
N.Y./ADAGP

The Tribe of Naphtali

1960–61, by Marc Chagall (Russian, 1887–1985). Final model for stained glass in Synagogue of Hadassah-Hebrew University Medical Center, Jerusalem. (The Granger Collection, New York). Copyright 1990 ARS N.Y./ADAGP

The Tribe of Zebulon

1960–61, by Marc Chagall (Russian, 1887–1985).
Stained glass window in Synagogue of Hadassah-
Hebrew University Medical Center, Jerusalem. (The
Granger Collection, New York). Copyright 1990 ARS
N.Y./ADAGP

Bride and Groom on a
Green Background

by Marc Chagall (Russian, 1887–1985). Christie's,
London. (Bridgeman/Art Resource, New York).
Copyright 1990 ARS N.Y./ADAGP

The Juggler of Paris

1969, by Marc Chagall (Russian, 1887–1985). The
Estate of Chagall, St. Paul de Vence. (Scala/Art
Resource, New York). Copyright 1990 ARS N.Y./ADAGP

Self Portrait

1959–68, by Marc Chagall (Russian, 1887–1985). Uffizi
Gallery, Florence. (Scala/Art Resource, New York).
Copyright 1990 ARS N.Y./ADAGP

Flowers against a Red Background

1970, by Marc Chagall (Russian, 1887–1985). The Estate of Chagall, St. Paul de Vence. (Scala/Art Resource, New York). Copyright 1990 ARS N.Y./ADAGP

In the Village

1973, by Marc Chagall (Russian, 1887–1985). The Estate of Chagall, St. Paul de Vence. (Scala/Art Resource, New York). Copyright 1990 ARS N.Y./ADAGP

Jacob's Ladder

1973, by Marc Chagall (Russian, 1887–1985). The
Estate of Chagall, St. Paul de Vence. (Scala/Art
Resource, New York). Copyright 1990 ARS N.Y./ADAGP

Still Life

1975, by Marc Chagall (Russian, 1887–1985). The
Estate of Chagall, St. Paul de Vence. (Scala/Art
Resource, New York). Copyright 1990 ARS N.Y./ADAGP

King David on a Red Background

1975, by Marc Chagall (Russian, 1887–1985). The
Estate of Chagall, St. Paul de Vence. (Scala/Art
Resource, New York). Copyright 1990 ARS N.Y./ADAGP

The Rider

1976, by Marc Chagall (Russian, 1887–1985). The
Estate of Chagall, St. Paul de Vence. (Scala/Art
Resource, New York). Copyright 1990 ARS N.Y./ADAGP

At the Circus

1976, by Marc Chagall (Russian, 1887–1985). The Estate of Chagall, St. Paul de Vence. (Scala/Art Resource, New York). Copyright 1990 ARS N.Y./ADAGP

Souvenir of the Magic Flute

1976, by Marc Chagall (Russian, 1887–1985). The
Estate of Chagall, St. Paul de Vence. (Scala/Art
Resource, New York). Copyright 1990 ARS N.Y./ADAGP

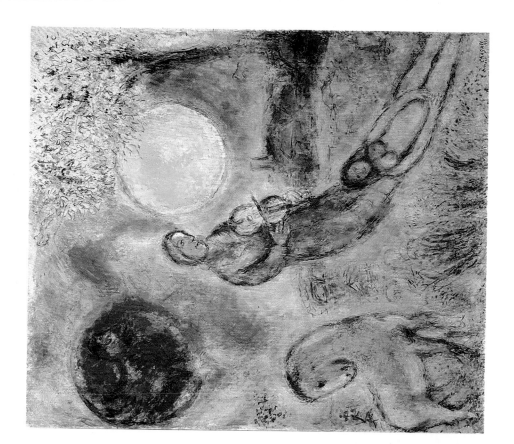

Cantique

1975–76, by Marc Chagall (Russian, 1887–1985). The Estate of Chagall, St. Paul de Vence. (Scala/Art Resource, New York). Copyright 1990 ARS N.Y./ADAGP